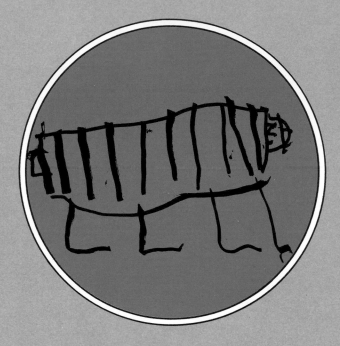

For Evan Miles Hunt
who drew this tiger

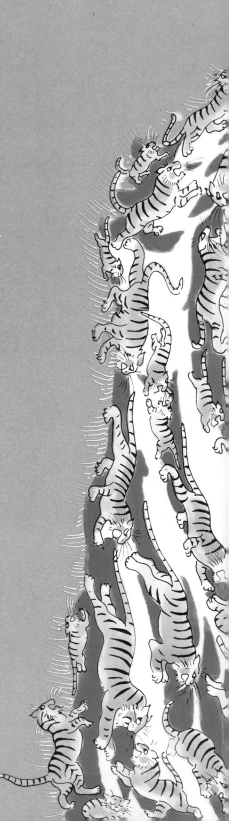

Publishers · Grosset & Dunlap · New York

Copyright © 1986 by Demi. All rights reserved. Published by Grosset &
Dunlap, Inc., a member of The Putnam Publishing Group, New York. Published
simultaneously in Canada. Printed in Hong Kong. Library of Congress Catalog
Card Number: 85-81653   ISBN 0-448-18980-1   B C D E F G H I J

1990 Paperback Edition   ISBN 0-448-19166-0

Here are the numbers you will need

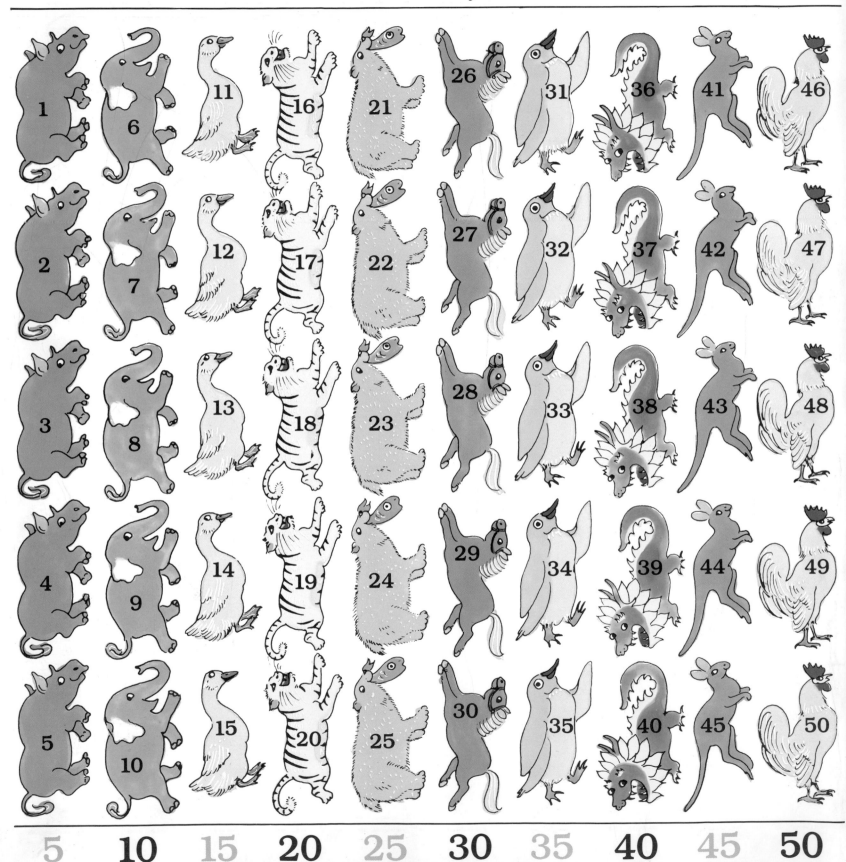

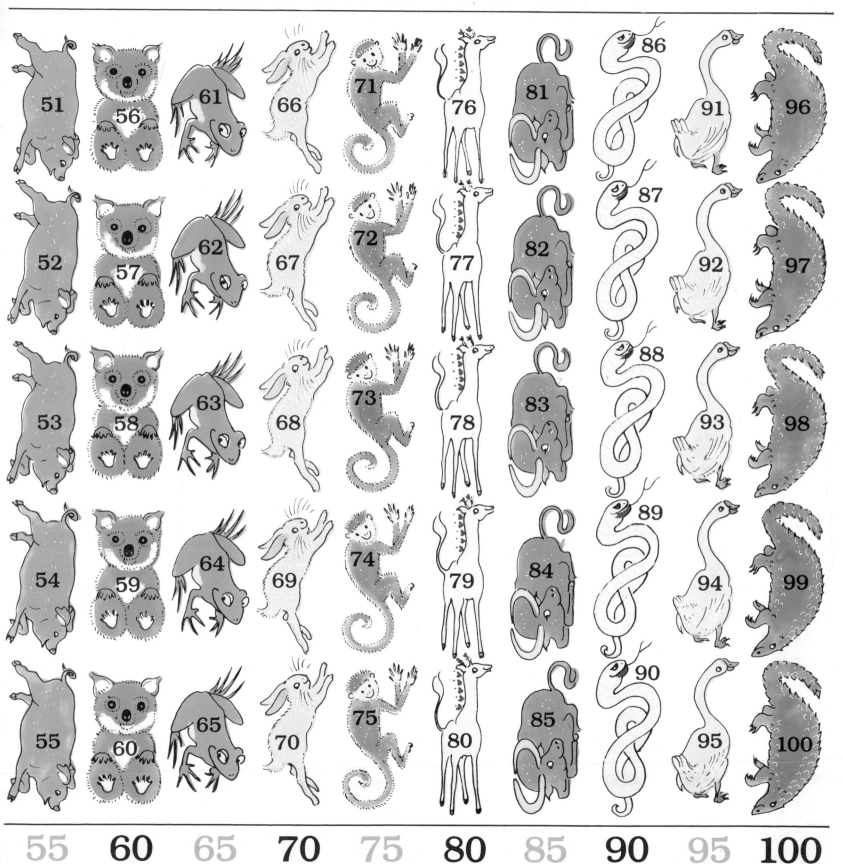

51 56 61 66 71 76 81 86 91 96

52 57 62 67 72 77 82 87 92 97

53 58 63 68 73 78 83 88 93 98

54 59 64 69 74 79 84 89 94 99

55 60 65 70 75 80 85 90 95 100

55 60 65 70 75 80 85 90 95 100

1
ONE

How many rhinos
on the run?
It's easy to see
there's only one.

Count one rhinoceros.

2
——
TWO

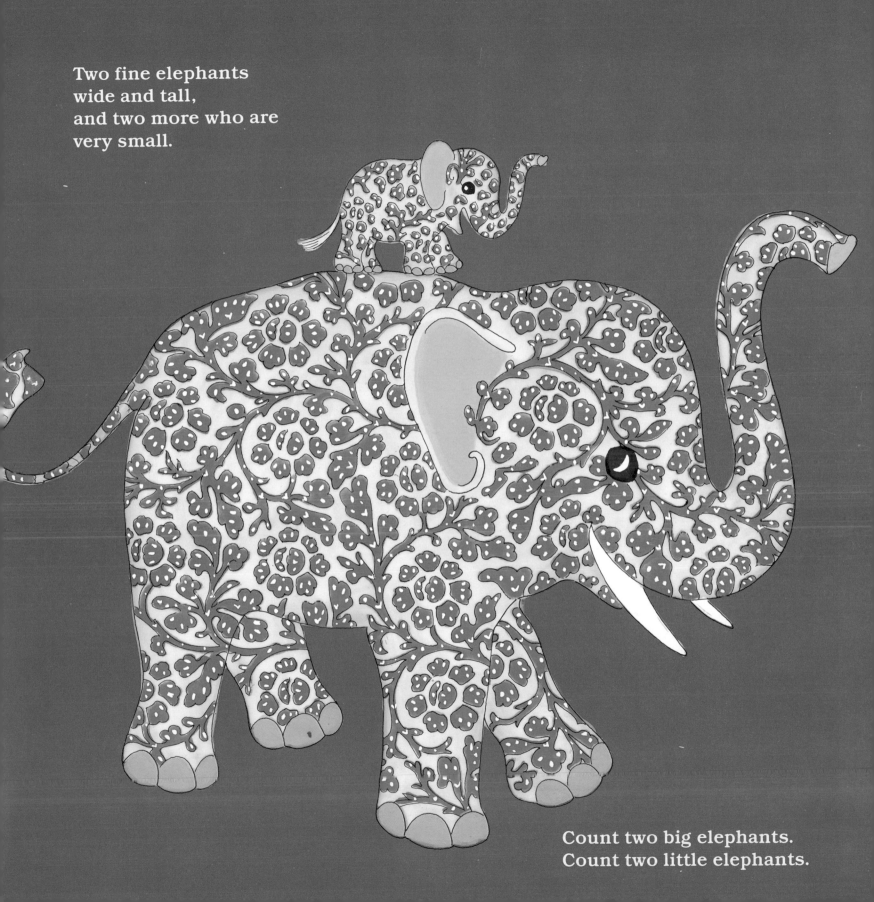

Two fine elephants
wide and tall,
and two more who are
very small.

Count two big elephants.
Count two little elephants.

3
THREE

Now we'll start
to count by threes,
baby ducks
and bumblebees.

Count three ducklings.
Count three worms,
    three flowers,
    and three bees.

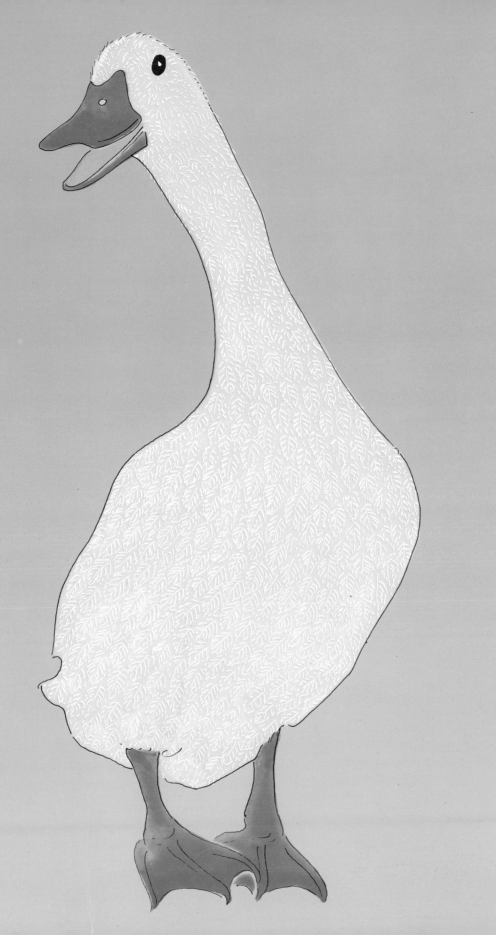

4
FOUR

Tigers race,
and tigers roar.
Now we're counting
up to four.

Count four tigers.
Count four tiger tails.

5
FIVE

Someone large
and gentle cares
for these five baby
polar bears.

Count five bear cubs.

6
SIX

How each prancing
pony kicks!
One, two, three,
four, five, and six!

Count six ponies.
Count six riders.

7
SEVEN

One by one,
the numbers grow.
Seven penguins
in a row.

Count seven penguins.
Count seven terns and seven fish.

8
EIGHT

Calling every
little dragon.
All aboard
the dragon-wagon!

Count eight little dragons.

9
NINE

Count one flowery
kangaroo.
Count nine little
joeys, too.

10
TEN

See the rooster.
See the hen.
Count the chicks
from one to ten.

11
ELEVEN

Eleven piglets,
pink and round.
One is falling
to the ground!

Count eleven
little piggies.

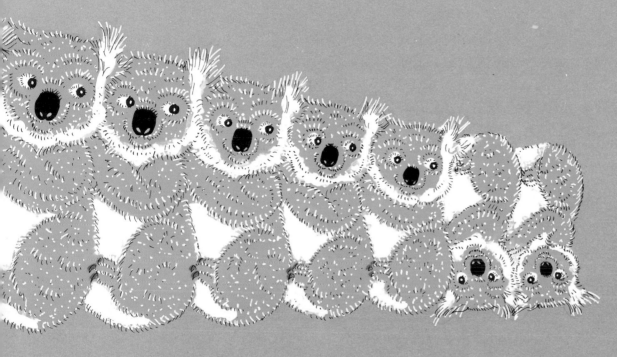

12
TWELVE

Each koala
hugs a cousin.
Soft koalas
by the dozen.

Count twelve koalas.
Count twelve black
koala noses.

13
THIRTEEN

See ten froggies
in the sun.
Add three more
for counting fun.

Count thirteen frogs.
Count thirteen flowers.

14
FOURTEEN

These rabbits may
be hard to count,
but fourteen is
the right amount.

Count fourteen rabbits.
Count fourteen snowflakes.

15
FIFTEEN

Stop and look.
There are fifteen
small monkeys here
that can be seen.

Count fifteen little monkeys.
Count fifteen bananas.

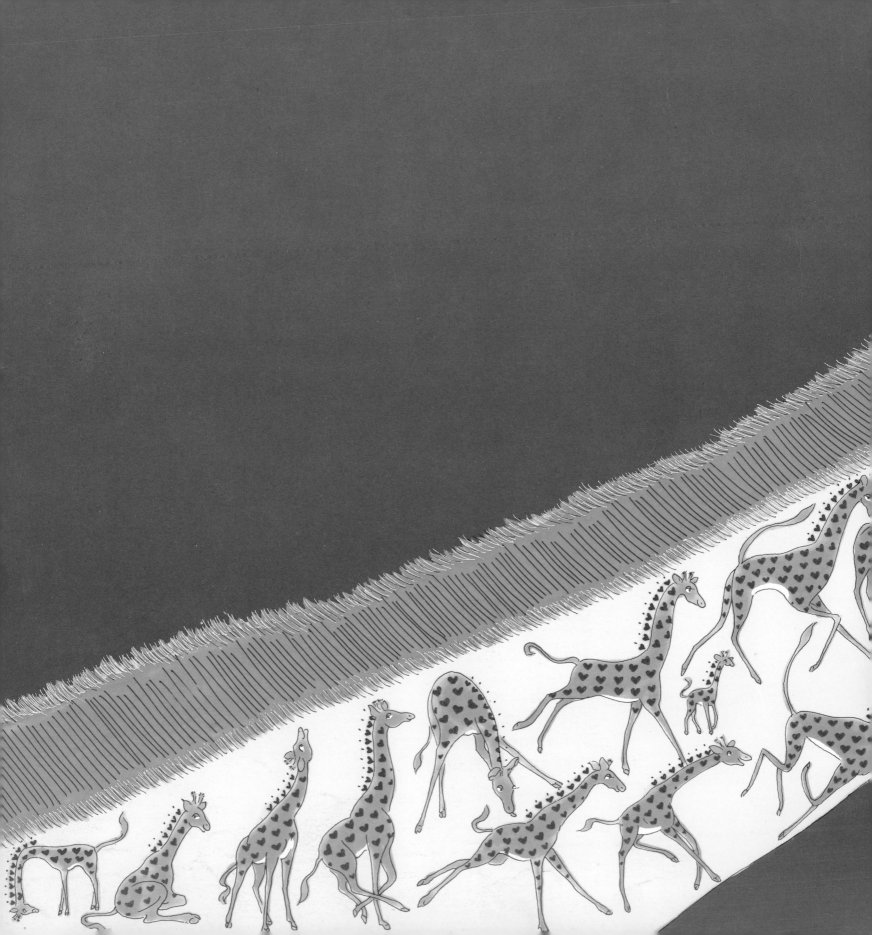

16
SIXTEEN

No more giggles.
No more laughs.
Just count sixteen
small giraffes.

17
SEVENTEEN

The stars that can
be clearly seen
add up to number
seventeen.

Count seventeen stars.
Count seventeen little
water buffaloes.

18
EIGHTEEN

Be careful! Wait—
before you pass.
A great big snake
lies in the grass.

Count eighteen little snakes.
Count eighteen blades of grass.

19
NINETEEN

Nineteen feathers
flying loose
belong to this
fine-feathered goose.

Count nineteen little geese.
Count nineteen feathers.

20

TWENTY

This pangolin
enjoys a treat.
Count twenty ants
he plans to eat!

Count twenty small pangolins.
Count twenty ants.

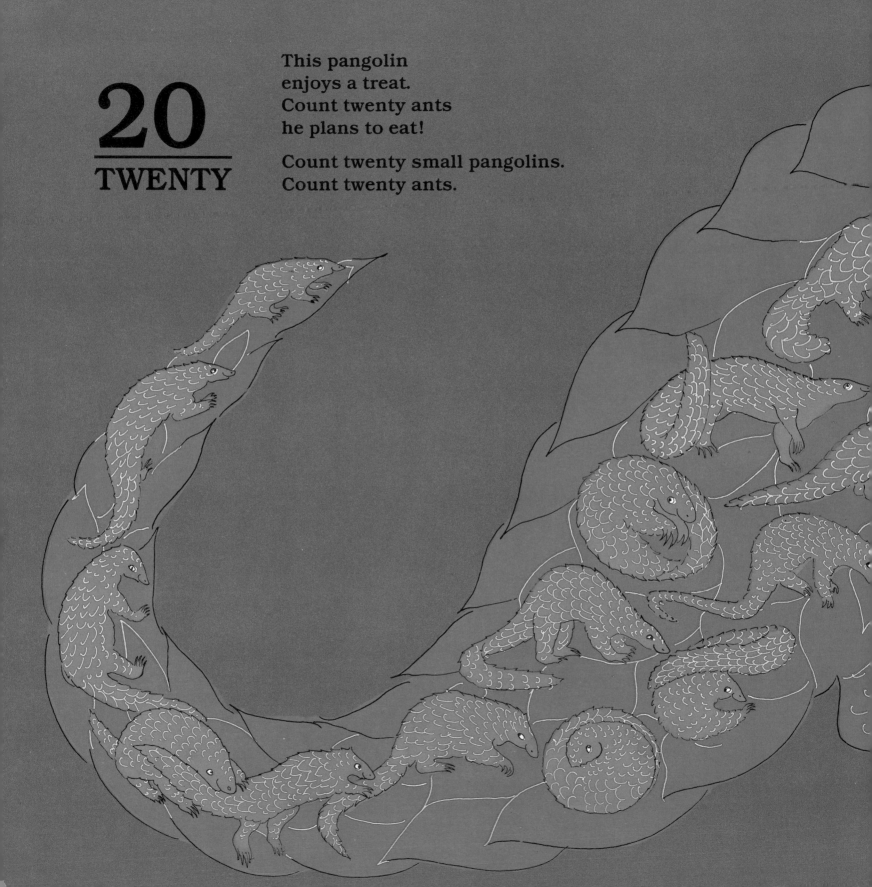

You can count to twenty. Now turn the page and try to count to one hundred.

COUNT ONE HUNDRED ANIMALS

TWO BY TWO ROUND AND ROUND